THE PASSION PLAY

DISCOVERING THE GOSPEL STORY AT OBERAMMERGAU

PETER WALKER

The Publisher shall take all necessary steps to secure copyright registration and protection of the Work in the English language. The right of Peter Walker to be identified as the author of this work shall be asserted in accordance with the Copyright, Designs and Patents Act 1988. The name of the Author shall appear with due prominence on the cover, spine, jacket (if any) and title page of every copy of the Work issued, unless previously agreed with the Proprietor. The following copyright notice shall appear:

The Passion Play: Discovering the Gospel Story at Oberammergau

All permission and other requests may be handled through our publisher website: www.
LeaderWorks.org/books
1080 Firewheel Lane, Prosper, Texas 75078

* * *

ISBN

Book Cover Design by David Roseberry
Printed in the United States of America

Created with Vellum

THE PASSION PLAY

DISCOVERING THE GOSPEL STORY AT OBERAMMERGAU

DR. PETER WALKER

CONTENTS

A NOTE FROM THE PUBLISHER

The Passion Play was first performed in Oberammergau in 1633. The tradition has been a once-in-a-decade occurrence ever since, and, up until last year, it didn't miss a scheduled performance. (Due to restrictions on travel, the play was postponed for three years during World War II.)

But, as we all know, the war years were not the only cause for postponing The Passion Play. The recent pandemic of 2020 was a terrible and ironic interruption.

The initial reason why The Passion Play was inaugurated in 1633 was to thank God for sparing the town from the ravages of the Black Plague in the early 1600s. In the Spring of 2020, the German government wisely decided to postpone this once-in-a-decade performance until 2022.

Undoubtedly, the government was aware of the sad irony of their decision. Some of Peter's remarks in the Preface, including comments he heard from the pastors in Oberammergau, express the sorrow that many in the Bavarian town felt when the news was released.

However, since we had some extra time to make further preparations for our rescheduled trips in 2022, Dr. Walker and I decided to team up and present this book to all potential and scheduled travelers for the 2022 showing of The Passion Play in Oberammergau.

You have that book in your hand now. You may call it a Field Guide. That is what it is. I would encourage you to read soon. And then read it on the plane to Germany in 2022, and then read through it the night before the drama begins.

Dr. Walker knows the play well, and we are indebted to him for his explanations and research about the Passion Play. He is a well qualified guide to historical play. With this book in your hand, you will understand the origins and the history of the performance itself. And, given what we have all lived through in 2020, the play's new dates make it all the more poignant to prepare.

But, as we know, the Passion of our Lord Jesus did not take place in Bavaria. It took place 2000 years ago in the historic City of David, Jerusalem. And Dr. Walker is eminently qualified to be our guide there too. Peter is a friend of mine. We met in Jerusalem in 1994 for the first time. And over the years, I have seen him produce written work, videos and lead tours to the Holy Land and through the ancient city of Jerusalem. Peter's book "In the Steps of Jesus: An Illustrated Guide to the Places of the Gospels" came out in 2006 and is the only book about the Holy Land that I have recommended for the over 30 tours that my wife and I have hosted on our own. And the good news is that he's just produced a fully revised, color edition for us to use on future tours![1]

Peter's love for the City of David and its history and struggles is well known. But also, Peter is a strongly committed Christian believer. He can be trusted to explain not only the mysteries of the ancient city but also the clear truths of the historic Christian faith.

I am very thankful to be able to publish this book. I plan to lead a trip to see The Passion Play in June of 2022 myself. I will ask every one of my travelers to read, mark, learn, and inwardly digest Peter's very helpful work here.

The Rev. Cn. David H. Roseberry
Ex. Director, LeaderWorks
Publisher, RMLBooks

PREFACE TO THE SECOND EDITION

By Peter Walker (Spring 2021)

When it came, though sadly expected, the news still triggered a wave of shock and grief: Oberammergau's Passion Play had been postponed for two years because of the coronavirus. It was late March 2020—just two months before the season's opening performances—and now all the extensive preparations were stopped in their tracks.

As the village's Lutheran pastor wrote to me a month later, "The grief over the postponement is deep." So much preparation—for example, "in the tailoring, the finishing of the decorations, the continuation of the scores and parts of voices"—had been so close to completion. People in the village had invested so much time and energy and had put other parts of their lives "on the back burner," he wrote. It was a "challenging and strange time."

Over the last four centuries, the decennial Play has been canceled twice (in 1770 and in 1940) and postponed three times (in 1800, 1810 and 1920). In the twentieth century, the interruptions were caused by two World Wars, but now the Play's delay is the same as that which triggered its very inception in 1634: a virulent plague.

Experiencing the threat of plague in 1633 in spite of their best attempts to place Oberammergau under strict quarantine, the villager's instincts were to pray earnestly for lives to be spared. They also returned their attention to the story of Jesus' suffering as recorded in the Gospels, in the hope of finding there a source of comfort in the midst of suffering.

That could be our response to the coronavirus pandemic in our own day. Looking ahead to an uncertain future, there may be wisdom in looking back to a fixed point, back to the drama and reality of an eight-day period that is better attested than any other week in the ancient world—a week which, in the eyes of many, was *the* pivotal game-changer in world history.

The story of Jesus—his innocent suffering and barbaric death followed by his being raised from the dead—continues to speak deeply into our human situation. We could see this undesired postponement of the Passion play, though bitterly disappointing, as an appropriate opportunity to once more to ponder the Passion of Jesus.

So, this second edition is being released as a resource for that opportunity, both to those who had been hoping to visit Oberammergau in 2020 and to those who perhaps had never even heard about the Passion Play. Chapter 2, "The Original Passion Story," is a retelling of history from the streets of first-century Jerusalem—so those wishing to focus on the Gospel records of Jesus' Passion might go straight there. (I have also produced an audio recording of that story, 'The Week that Changed the World," available for live streaming at walkwaybooks.com.)

Others, however, might want to approach the story through chapter 1, "Setting the Scene," allowing the village of Oberammergau to act as an "avenue" into the story, thus preparing to experience the Passion with a sensitivity both to its drama and to its potential impact on human beings in times of uncertainty. Chapter 3 is an exploration of the Old Testament *tableaus* (or "living images") that frame the Passion play, giving us greater depths of understanding about what Jesus was doing within the overall biblical story.

I am so grateful for those in Oberammergau who offered me hospitality during the summer of 2019, and especially to those I interviewed who shared so openly what was on their hearts. This edition is dedicated to them with deep gratitude. I hope this small book may help many more people to appreciate the great gift they offer to the worldwide community in this difficult season of suffering and confusion.

A WARM WELCOME TO OBERAMMERGAU

HERZLICH WILLKOMMEN!

Before, during, and after the Passion Play a warm welcome awaits you in the village of Oberammergau.

To be immersed in the story of Jesus' life and death for more than five hours in a day is, for most visitors, a unique experience in their lives—sometimes even overwhelming. New thoughts come to mind, emotions are stirred, and many need time to think through and to process all they have thought and felt.

That's why we in the village's Catholic and Lutheran parishes, working together as an ecumenical team, are developing opportunities each day during the Passion Play season for visitors to continue with their thoughts and reflections. In the center of the village, for example, there will be an open space in the so-called *Sternplatz* ("Place of the Star") that will highlight themes such as trust, fear, and resurrection—all designed to help people make connections between the story of the Passion and their own lives.

Moreover, on each performance day (Sunday, Tuesday, Thursday, Friday, and Saturday) the village's churches will offer services and other events:

- The Catholic Church of St. Peter and Paul is located on Ettaler Straße.
- The Lutheran Kreuzkirche ("Church of the Cross") is located 100-yards east of the theater on Theaterstraße.

In all of these places, there will be people from the village who are willing to talk or assist in any way that might be helpful. We hope visitors will experience not just open doors but open hearts. For we truly want people to have a full "Oberammergau experience"—not just seeing the Passion Play but allowing it to have its full effect. Please enjoy being in our village, drink in its atmosphere and experience our hospitality.

We read in the Gospels of the welcome Jesus himself gave to the crowds: When Jesus saw a large crowd, he had compassion on them, because they were like sheep without a shepherd. So, he began to teach them many things (Mark 6:34).

As people entrusted with pastoral care within our local church community, we are aware of our privilege in being available to come alongside people from all over the world with a wide variety of backgrounds and beliefs—and in being able to listen in an open-hearted way to whatever our visitors share. "Compassion" means literally to "suffer alongside someone" or to "go through an experience together." That's what we seek to do in Oberammergau: We hope to come alongside our visitors to experience the Passion together.

Our motto as an ecumenical team, *Leidenschaft Lebe,* is based on the words for "passion" and "life." In English, as in German, there are some double meanings in the word "passion." One can speak of someone having a "life passion"; one can speak of someone experiencing a "passionate life" or "living a life of compassion." There are different shades of meaning.

There is a sense in which coming to Oberammergau turns out for many to be a pilgrimage. Whatever their original motivation, people find it becomes in some way a journey of faith, helping them move forward through their lives with a new sense of direction, a clearer purpose, and a deeper understanding. For some, it is expressly a time for discovering or rediscovering what it can mean to walk along the way of Jesus, to live one's life "the Jesus way."

Our hope and prayer is that your visit to Oberammergau, as you give a day of your life to being immersed in the Passion, will indeed help you to return to your home with a new vision for living out the story of Jesus and for being recognized as a person who has been marked by your experience of his Passion.

Faithfully yours,,

Pastor Peter Sachi

Pastor, Evangelisch-Lutherische Kirchengemeinde),

Father Thomas Gröner
Parish Priest

Dr. Angela Winterer
Pastoral Coworker, Katholische Pfarrgemeinde
Oberammergau)

If you or your group would like to be in touch with us during your visit to Oberammergau, contact us at:

http://oberammergau-evangelisch.de

HOW TO USE THIS BOOK

You have this book in your hand because you are interested in the Passion Play being performed in Oberammergau, Germany. It is good to start thinking about all this—given the time it takes us normally to prepare for such events in our lives but, even more so now, given the long months of time that have passed during the Play's postponement. I hope you are starting to feel excited. You should be! It will be well worth the wait.

And this handy guide can be your companion from now on—as well as on the plane and during the day of the performance.

Four Sections

The book is set up in four sections. The first section gives the background to the events described in the Bible surrounding the last three days of Jesus' life. We also look at the profound impact of those events on subsequent history.

The second section will look in detail at the absorbing history of Passion Play as it has been performed in Oberammergau through the centuries and now in our own day. I think you will be fascinated by the amazing commitment shown by this small town in hosting this massive spectacle.

The third section will walk you through the biblical scenes in the four Gospels. Many of us learn the story of the last three days of Jesus' life in scattered bits and pieces, but here it is laid out for you in a chronological sequence—hour by hour.

There are twelve acts, and they correspond to the sequence of Acts or Scenes in the Passion Play itself. However, the Oberammergau performance only has eleven Acts, leaving the audience in front of an empty tomb.

It is indeed a powerful moment, leaving the audience on tiptoe with a sense of hope and longing. In my opinion, however, it is not enough! There is so much more to the life of Jesus than just an empty tomb. According to all the New Testament writers, he was raised bodily from the grave to a new and vibrant life, appearing to more than five hundred followers over a period of some forty days (see Acts 1:3; 1 Cor. 15:3-8). And this means he is alive today! So, I do hope you will not mind this last addition—it is in your Bible!

Finally, the last part of this book contains a description of twelve tableau from the Old Testament. A tableau is a dramatic device used in theatrical performances to provide emphasis or background. Usually, there is no action in a tableau: it is a static pose or 'snapshot', capturing one critical moment in time.

Each of the twelve tableau that you will see plays an integral and important role within the Passion Play. And, as you will see, they are all based on vivid scenes from the Old Testament, giving us a deeply biblical lens through which we can see how the events unfolding in Jesus' life had been prefigured in the lives of God's people many centuries before. Jesus was fulfilling and bringing to a climax a story that God had been carefully writing ever since his call to Abraham.

Reading my explanation and then closely observing the characters in the tableaus will hopefully prove true the insight of St. Augustine: "*The New Testament is in the Old Testament concealed; the Old Testament is in the New Testament revealed.*" In other words, the Old Testament stories were profound previews of the work of the Messiah—containing hidden truths which only his arrival in human history would bring fully into the light.

So, my hope is that this last section of your book will help you to sense the unfathomable depths that lie behind the Passion story—as well as helping you to engage yourself with the story that God is writing in each of our lives.

1

THE PASSION OF OUR LORD JESUS

A "drop in the ocean"? Is that what we are dealing with when we turn to consider the story of Jesus of Nazareth and his death in Jerusalem—something small and insignificant? Or is it more like a large boulder, dropped from a great height, pounding into the streets below—something powerful in its impact and long-lasting in its repercussions?

When something is dropped, its overall effect is a combination of *what* is dropped—its identity—and *where* it is dropped—its location. Given that we are still talking about it 2000 years later, the Passion Story, which traces the events leading up to Jesus' crucifixion, has had an effect quite disproportionate to what one might have expected: Why on earth are we still talking about the death of a Jewish teacher so many years after all his contemporaries are long since dead and gone?

Because of who Jesus was—his identity—and where his dramatic story took place—his location.

It turns out that Jerusalem was no ordinary place. Instead, it was a city at the center of an ancient story, going back millennia, full of promise and claiming to be the true story at the center of the whole world.

And Jesus was no ordinary character. Instead, he was a person who, bolstered by his fine teaching and apparent acts of incredible power, claimed to be the long-awaited central character in that ancient story. It was this combination—the arrival of *this* Jesus in *this* Jerusalem—that caused sparks to fly. The coming of Jesus was like a great and mighty stone dropped from a vast height; his coming to *Jerusalem* meant the stone was about to land at a key center in the ancient world. No wonder we are still feeling the ripple effect.

This is one reason—among many others—that a small Bavarian village is still performing its world-famous Passion Play every 10 years for nearly four centuries. Quite an incredible achievement on the part of a small village! And, although at one level a play performed by rural villagers seems to be fairly insignificant—just another "drop in the ocean"—at another level, it is an extraordinary phenomenon, with an impact disproportionate to its actual size. Asking why this is so, one might conclude that the story it seeks to retell is at the epicenter of the entire world.

THE BACKGROUND OF THE PASSION STORY

Jerusalem at the time of Jesus was a city of around 20,000 inhabitants. At an elevation of nearly 3,000 feet above sea level and located on a line of hills forming a central spine down the length of the country, from Samaria in the north to Hebron in the south, it was a city to which all visitors had to "go up"—whether from the Mediterranean coastal plain to the west or from the Jordan valley and the Dead Sea to the east.

Founded by Israel's most famous king, David, and centered around the magnificent Temple first built by his son, Solomon, Jerusalem had been at the center of Israel's life for just over a thousand years—through the turbulent centuries of the kingdom ruled by David's heirs, through the dark days of Babylonian captivity and exile, through the era of the Temple's restoration and some years of joyful independence—but was now under enemy occupation. Jerusalem had shrunk to a shadow of its former self—now seemingly a small, insignificant place on the remote eastern borders of the vast and brutal Roman empire.

So much history, so much hope—but now, so much pain.

According to the Hebrew Scriptures (often referred to as the Old Testament), Jerusalem was the setting for three annual religious festivals, one of which (Passover) celebrated the dramatic emancipation in the days of Moses of the Hebrew slaves from under the yoke of Egypt's powerful ruler, the pharaoh. Not surprisingly, when Jerusalem's streets were crowded with Passover pilgrims—sometimes numbering over a million, according to the Jewish historian, Josephus—tensions could run high. The pilgrims longed for a new Moses, a new David, a new restorer of the Temple, a new king—any or all of the above, if only they could somehow get rid of the hated Romans!

So much religious longing, so much ardent praying, and so much political tension. Jerusalem was like an oil tanker cruising on a seething wave of volcanic lava: only one small spark and the whole thing could go up in flames.

It was into this prime location—this well-primed pressure-cooker, if you like—that Jesus walked, advancing his own purposes and announcing his surprising identity. People had begun to wonder if he was indeed the Messiah—the Hebrew term for the "anointed" king whom they hoped would re-establish David's independent kingdom. What if they were right?

The Passion story is the story of what happened when the dynamic energy of Jesus' unique character encountered the pent-up frustrations and longings that were woven into the very fabric of Jerusalem. It's a story about *his identity* in *this location*. That's the combination that gives the story its power.

THE IMPACT OF THE PASSION STORY

Imagine now that you and I tried to explain this background to visitors from Mars. They might conclude, "So Jesus, if he was indeed the Davidic king, stormed into Jerusalem and routed the Romans! Have we got that right?"

Imagine their puzzled expressions when we reply, "No. Within a week Jesus was dead, put to death as a political agitator by those brutish Romans."

Most likely they would reply, "So obviously, he was *not* the king. End of story! And we can't work out why you're still talking about this dead-end story 2,000 years later. There's no story here worth telling!"

Our Martian visitors' logic is compelling. But we have not told them the whole story. The writers of the four Gospels—the original sources for the story of Jesus—all affirm that the story did not end with Jesus' death. Something happened a few days later that flipped the whole story, transforming it from a tale of tragedy into a journey of joy. In musical terms, the composer's score suddenly shifted from a minor key to the major. Hope was vindicated. "There was a sudden and unexpected twist in the storyline," we tell our Martian visitors. "And that's why we're still talking about it so many years later."

The impact of the Jesus story depends—perhaps more than we often realize—on the story of the Resurrection, the claim that he was raised physically from the dead. Without that ingredient in the story, there is simply no reason why anyone—whether in first-century Jerusalem, seventeenth-century Oberammergau, or the contemporary world—would still be talking about it. Indeed, we might never even have heard the name "Jesus of Nazareth." For why tell a story about a rural villager going up to a big city with some grandiose ideas but who gets crushed by the system?

The Gospel writers—Matthew, Mark, Luke, and John—though they tell the story with slightly different colors and from different angles and perspectives, are united in their motivation: This story *must* be told because it is not just a true story about bad things that happen to good people. It is also a true story about what the God of Israel did through this Jesus among his people—fully in keeping with their long-cherished hopes but also exceeding and transforming those hopes in many ways.

Moreover, they must tell this story because, though it is a Jewish story, it is also more. Jesus walked, as it were, into the storyline of Israel, moved the plot forward, and then—through the dramatic "sting in the tail" of his Resurrection—blew the story wide open, so that it could now, at last, go out to the wider world. He "came to his own people," wrote John at the start of his Gospel. Yet he was also "coming into the world" in order to "give light" to a world shrouded in darkness. John wrote with the hope that his readers—wherever they were in the world—would come to see that what Jesus did in Jerusalem was indeed done for them and could transform their own worlds from darkness to light and from tragedy to joy.

Jesus' Passion was the climax of an age-long larger story recorded in the Hebrew scriptures, a multigenerational story about one small people-group chosen to become a blessing to all nations with a message of good news from Jerusalem to the ends of the earth. The Jesus story is the hinge on which the whole plot turns, at the epicenter of divine purposes and set against a universal backdrop. It was—and indeed still is—a story *of* the world and *for* the world. It is the story, as many have claimed, that lies at the very center of all human history.

This was the story's impact as it was felt in the first century. And that's why the story has been told ever since—through the eras of the Roman and Byzantine empires, through the so-called "Dark Ages" and the Medieval period, through the last 400 years in Oberammergau and now all around the globe.

2

THE ORIGINS OF THE PASSION PLAY AT OBERAMMERGAU

"There's no place like home!" Sometimes the desire to return to the place of one's upbringing and to be with one's own family is irresistible. So must have felt a young man called Kaspar Schisler, who for several months had been working on a farm in a Bavarian village called Eschenlohe, about 10 miles from Oberammergau.

The year was 1632. The horrendous Thirty Years' War, which would ultimately take the lives of millions, had ravaged across Europe for the last 10 years and had brought in its wake a deadly pestilence—almost certainly the bubonic plague. Oberammergau's sheltered location, surrounded by so many hills, had enabled the village to be spared thus far, but special precautionary measures had been taken: All people entering the valley were to be placed in quarantine. Thus the plague was kept at bay—until Kaspar, longing to be at home for Easter, sneaked in by night.

A few days later he would be dead, his family infected. In due course, as can be seen today in the Parish Register of deaths (the *Pestmatrikel*), some 80 or more villagers would lose their lives. In this dire situation, the leaders of the village came together in the church: "The village councils met," so the local chronicle attests, "and vowed to perform the Passion play every ten years; and from this time on not a single person more died." Standing in front of the crucifix—which still stands on the righthand side in the Catholic parish church—they made this solemn vow, which has continued to be fulfilled to this day.

Such a vow might seem odd to us. Did they really think that such an act of penitence might avert the plague? And why choose the performance of the Passion as their mode of penitence? On the latter point, we can note that Passion plays had something of a popular resurgence during the previous hundred years in the Catholic heartland of southern Germany and Austria. Such plays had started in the twelfth century, with many cities across Europe, including Chester and Coventry in England, putting on plays during Holy Week. They reached their peak of popularity around 1500 but then fell out of favor. In rural Bavaria, however, they came back into vogue as a vital part of the Catholic Church, reinvigorating the faith of its members. One can imagine how the village leaders might make this decision: In their circumstances of suffering and fear, there might be great comfort and consolation in contemplating what was endured by Jesus, the one they believed to have been none other than the Son of God.

The following May, in 1634, villagers gathered in the church's graveyard to watch more than 60 of their fellow residents perform the first-ever Oberammergau Passion Play—"the play of the suffering, death and resurrection of our Lord Jesus Christ."

It has continued ever since. The sixth Passion Play was rescheduled to be performed at the start of the new decade in 1680. During the eighteenth century, the so-called "Age of Reason," the village had to request permission from political leaders to perform such a religious act; this led to performances sometimes being delayed by a year or, as in 1770, banned altogether. Wars have also affected the sequence: There was an interrupted season in 1870 and 1871 due to war with France, a delayed performance in 1922 because of the First World War, and no performance at all in 1940 thanks to World War Two. On the other hand, there have occasionally been extra seasons: in 1815, after the end of the Napoleonic Wars, and in 1934 and 1984 to honor the three-hundredth and three-hundred-fiftieth anniversaries of the Play.

In 2022 the Play will be in its forty-second season, making it one of the longest-running theatrical performances of all time!

This powerful history makes Oberammergau unique both for its visitors and for its residents. Visitors are introduced to all the charms of a rural Bavarian village—historic buildings, local shops, places to eat and drink, set amid a beautiful surrounding countryside—but also to something more. The village, deeply immersed in the Passion for nearly 400 years, is indelibly colored by this history.

For example, the common Bavarian practice of painting the outside walls of one's house with frescoes (*luftmalerei* in German) has here been given a biblical twist. Yes, there are frescoes depicting figures from traditional nursery rhymes, such as those on the Hansel and Gretel House, but many depict biblical characters—for example, those on the building known as Pilate's House and those on a chemist's shop where the eighteenth-century owner left for passersby an impressive display of characters from the pages of the Bible and the history of the Church.

And then there is the prominence of woodcarving in the village. If Bethlehem can claim to be the unrivaled center of woodcarving in the Holy Land today, much the same can be said for Oberammergau in Europe. The village supports more than 500 woodcarvers. Bethlehem is immersed in the Nativity and Oberammergau in the Passion.

The sheer number of visitors also makes the village unique. The worldwide fame of the Passion Play inspires tourists to visit year and year out, but the number escalates exponentially during performance seasons: With 4,500 people in the audience for each of five weekly performances, and with many of those wanting to stay the night, Oberammergau brims to capacity.

What does it feel like to have your small town invaded once every 10 years by people from around the world? And what does it mean to live in a community constantly "under the shadow"—even if in very positive ways—of the Passion story? How does it feel to go on stage with your fellow villagers and play a small part in the Palm Sunday procession or to take one of the 20 main roles, including those of Jesus' mother and Mary Magdalene—or of Jesus himself?

Living in Oberammergau thus presents its residents with unique experiences. It was my privilege to talk with some of them during my research for this book. Yes, there are some who have little direct involvement with the Play and don't see it affecting their everyday life all that much; others who admit they stand at some distance from the Christian faith; and still others who, while intrigued by the story of Jesus, are in a critical ongoing dialogue with the Church.

On the other hand, there are those who see the Passion Play as an opportunity to help people enter more deeply into the story of the Gospels. I particularly enjoyed meeting Dr. Angelika Winterer, a theologian appointed by the local Catholic archbishop with special responsibility for pastoral care and counsel before and during the Passion Play season. By 2019 she was already taking people on meditative journeys—through guided reading, short talks, and shared photos of the Holy Land—to the places and stories described in the Gospels. She was leading visitors on guided tours around the church (some focused on the *Pestmatrikel*, the Parish Register of Deaths from 1633, as mentioned above). All these activities are designed to help people connect the Passion story more deeply with their own personal lives.

"Visiting the Passion Play," she told me, "can strengthen people in their faith. This is because the Play tells us how God did not leave Jesus alone in the terrible distress of the Passion but ultimately led him through suffering and death to resurrection and life. Moreover, it reminds us how the people of Oberammergau also experienced God's salvation in 1633. Similar experiences can be had by people time and again: They can receive help and assistance whenever they trust in

God in their time of need. For this reason, the Passion Play can, I truly believe, bring consolation and support, courage, and hope—especially to those who themselves are going through a period of suffering or difficulty."

STAGING THE PASSION AT OBERAMMERGAU

Writing the script for a modern comedy or fictional drama is no easy task, but the challenges are amplified when one seeks to portray an event from history. How does one ensure the performance is true to the facts when it is a *performance*, an artificial and slightly contrived creation?

Matters become even more complex when you're writing about more distant events from history. Hundreds of years later, we know just the top-level facts. All we can see at this distance is the tip of an iceberg; most of the original history—what was really happening "on the streets"—now lies buried out of view. How can you help the audience imagine themselves inside such an ancient story? You will have to write something that is humanly credible and makes sense—even though, strictly speaking, it will be a work of fiction. The only way to convey historical truth on stage is to write a script based on imagination. Indeed, imagination is the only way a script can become authentic to the experience of the audience. That's how it *becomes real.*

The audience must be taken on an imaginary journey of time-travel going back 2,000 years. They need to be transported from the modern world into the ancient Roman Empire—and indeed into a strange, smaller "sub-world" within that Empire: the world of first-century Judaism. How can they step into the sandals of a first-century Jew? There is a real challenge here when it comes to helping people adjust their mindsets.

Despite the distance in time, however, there is one striking advantage for a Passion play: We know far more about that week in Jerusalem than any other week in ancient history. It's not just that we have good archaeological evidence of first-century Jerusalem and good sources for what Passover celebrations would have been like. We also have four accounts of what happened on Sunday, Monday, Thursday, Friday, and the following Sunday! Moreover, the story is told from the perspectives not of later imperial historians, but of real people on the ground. In other words, we know what was being talked about "on the streets"!

Yet this comparative wealth of down-to-earth information can also cause some difficulties for the scriptwriter of a Passion play. For a start, given that there are four different Gospels, does one give preference to one of those four accounts and its particular angle on Jesus? And, although we know the names of some of the ordinary "bit players," such as Peter and Thomas and Mary, we can often only guess what they were feeling as they went through these dramatic events. By necessity, the scriptwriter is still going to have to embellish the original accounts.

At that point, one runs into another difficulty. This particular story is sacred to so many; the very language of the original accounts has become canonical and revered. How can one add to the Bible—the historic script—without in some way undermining it? Many in the audience will be familiar with the story or even devoted to it, seeing it as a foundational story of their faith and spirituality. How can one help them discover new and even shocking insights into the original story without causing offense?

Other theatrical works may present challenges for how to convey authentic history in an imaginable and authentic way, but here there are issues that touch on spiritual faith and personal commitments. A Passion play, by its very nature, can never be *only* about history. It necessarily brushes that most divisive of subjects: theology. For the Gospel writers were not just "bare historians," so to speak; they were committed Christian believers. They told a story that was not just historically true but, for them, theologically extraordinary.

The scriptwriter of a Passion play must juggle these inevitable issues of theology. For example, if the Gospel writers advance the claim that Jesus was not just a remarkable human being but also mysteriously embodied the character of Israel's God, how can a Passion play give appropriate space for that conclusion to be drawn? Must the focus be solely on the historical Jesus, or can the script include words that point to the divinity of Jesus? If the Gospel writers assert that this historical Jesus was physically raised from the dead, how does one portray such a miracle on stage? Or is it best to convey this idea in more symbolic ways, giving space for the audience to draw their own conclusions?

For nearly 400 years, those producing the Passion Play in Oberammergau have been wrestling with these and similar issues. In the early years, there were issues to do with blending Catholic and Reformed perspectives on the Passion. In 1730, allegorical characters were introduced by the Augustinian Anselm Manhart, setting the Passion story against the backdrop of a battle between Jesus and Satan (together with his minions Jealousy, Avarice, Sin, and Death). During the Age of Reason, the play went in a different, more meditative, direction and began to include the *tableaux vivants*. In the 1810s, a new script by Othmar Weiss eliminated any allegorical elements, focused on the realism of the gospels, used prose rather than verse, and began to highlight moral issues such as social injustice. In 1860, the text was revised yet again by Josef Alois Daisenberger, who focused more on idealism and on the psychological elements in the story. More than 100 years later, Daisenberger's text is still being used, but care is now taken to ensure it is free from anti-Semitism that was so tragically common to earlier eras.

Through the past four centuries, the script has been influenced by the important concerns of each successive time period—concerns both in the Christian Church and also in the wider world of politics and philosophy. Each scriptwriter has sought to make fresh and vital connections between this ancient story and the contemporary world. The script continues to evolve as it travels down the line of human history.

Let's dive deeper into the historical events that anchor each scriptwriter's creative labors.

3

THE FIRST PASSION STORY

What follows is a retelling of the original Passion story, based on accounts in the four Gospels and set against what we now know about its historical background.

The story is told here in twelve installments, arranged roughly according to their chronology. As mentioned above (in 'How to Use this Book), the final installment has been added because of our conviction that the fuller story of Jesus' Resurrection, as found in the Gospels and proclaimed by the Christian Church ever since, should not be omitted—even if we concede that it might indeed be problematic to present this unique event in history convincingly on a stage.

The first eleven installments, however, follow exactly the eleven Acts as performed on the stage in Oberammergau. As such they are probably worth reading through in the last few days before your own attendance at the Play; for there certainly will not be time to attempt reading them once the Play begins! Yet they are designed to give you the assurance, as you are watching the Play being performed in German, that what you are seeing—even if obviously 'staged' and in that sense 'artificial'—is nevertheless based on solid and reliable history, grounded in what took place on the streets of Jerusalem 2000 years ago.

	Event	Day / Time
1.	Jesus enters Jerusalem	Sunday
2.	Jesus in Bethany	Monday–Wednesday
3.	Jesus cleanses the Temple	Monday
4.	Jesus shares a meal with his followers	Thursday, 6 PM
5.	Jesus in Gethsemane	Thursday, 10 PM
6.	Jesus on trial before Caiaphas	Friday, 3 AM
7.	Jesus encounters human evil and failure	Friday, 3 AM
8.	Jesus on trial before Pontius Pilate and Herod	Friday, 6 AM
9.	Jesus is sentenced to death	Friday, 8 AM
10.	Jesus is crucified	Friday, 10 AM
11.	Jesus appears to Mary Magdalene	Sunday, 6 AM
12.	Jesus appears to his followers	Sunday, 6 PM

These events comprise the most famous week in history. Unlike any other span of days in the ancient world, we know something of what happened on almost every single day of the week. The days and times listed above, however, remain somewhat uncertain. In recent years there has been some debate about the Jewish calendar—on which day of the week did Passover fall that year? —and what that might mean for the Last Supper. Perhaps, it has been suggested, that meal took place on Tuesday or Wednesday? And perhaps Jesus was placed in prison for one or more nights before his crucifixion on Friday morning?

In this retelling we assume the traditional dating of the Last Supper on Thursday evening. That particular year the Passover meal would have been celebrated by everyone else on the Friday evening, but tradition says Jesus held his own "Passover" a day ahead of schedule because he knew that, 24 hours later, he would be dead.

There is also uncertainty about the first half of the week. For example, Jesus' entrance into the city may well have fallen on Sunday, the first day of the Jewish week. After observing a sabbath rest in Jericho on Saturday, he and the other Galileans could have set out on Sunday morning and reached Jerusalem in the late afternoon. Hence the note in Mark's Gospel that after Jesus had entered the Temple, "he looked around at everything but, since it was already late, he went out to Bethany with the Twelve" (11:11). In the next verse Mark then talks about "the next day" (that is, Monday), indicating that was the day Jesus cursed the fig tree and then stormed into the Temple, driving out the moneychangers (vv. 15-18). However, both of these entrances into the Temple might have taken place one day later (Monday and Tuesday).

The Oberammergau script is divided into 11 acts. Each of the first 11 installments below, then, can act as useful historical background to the corresponding act's performance, serving as a reminder that the drama unfolding onstage is not a mythical tale but based on events that actually happened on the streets of first-century Jerusalem.

Below, however, an additional and final installment has been added. This is because the Oberammergau Passion Play leaves the viewer at the empty tomb, rather than continuing the fuller story found in the Gospels that describes events later on that Sunday—not least, Jesus' reunion with his disciples in the upper room. The narrative here thus gives you the whole story, from Palm Sunday through the end of Easter Sunday: eight full days that, taken together, can rightly claim to have changed the history of the world.

1. JESUS ENTERS JERUSALEM

They say that, to this day, the Jewish heart when it catches the first sighting of Jerusalem misses a beat—such is the Jewish depth of affection for this city at the center of their national story.

And so, it would have been on that memorable day when Jesus made his so-called 'Triumphal Entry." The many Galilean pilgrims, who had been walking for the last week in Jesus' company, would have had a rush of instinctive joy and delight when—at last—they came over the crest of the Mount of Olives and saw the beauty of their mother city spread out before their eyes.

When he came near the place where the road goes down the Mount of Olives, the whole crowd of disciples began joyfully to praise God in loud voices for all the miracles they had seen: "Blessed is the king who comes in the name of the Lord!" "Peace in heaven and glory in the highest!" (Luke 19:37–38).

The last part of their journey had been a long climb through the desert, coming up from Jericho—near the Dead Sea, the lowest place on the face of the planet—to Jerusalem, more than 2,700 feet above sea level. Presumably, they had set out at the break of dawn in order to cover the necessary 14 miles in one day. Not surprisingly, we read in Mark's Gospel that by the time Jesus reached Jerusalem it was "already late" in the afternoon. [1]It had been a long day, and they would have been tired but also filled with a sense of arrival and expectation. Now they could settle down and start preparing for the Passover festival!

Yet, this particular year, they also had other reasons for their excitement. For they all had high hopes for this Jesus figure, this powerful teacher from Nazareth, this prophet in their midst. Might some sparks begin to fly once they hit Jerusalem?! Luke expressly says there were many among the pilgrims setting out from Jericho who thought, as Jesus entered Jerusalem, that the "kingdom of God was going to appear at once" [2]. They were on tiptoe with expectation. Might this be the year when, through this Jesus, God's kingly rule over Israel might be restored? Would those hated oppressors, the Romans, at last be removed from the land?

Jesus himself, however, seemed to have other ideas. As they set out through the Judean desert, he told them a parable about a king coming back to his own country and judging those who during his absence had rebelled at his rule.[3] What was he driving at? The idea of

Jesus as a king was indeed good news, but why did he describe his coming as a "return"? And why was he speaking about judgment?

And then, when they came up with the final slopes of the Mount of Olives, Jesus requisitioned a donkey from the nearby village of Bethany. Why a donkey and not something more impressive? Why not a horse or a mighty stallion? If the Romans ever heard about this supposed king approaching on a silly donkey, they would be moved to pitiful laughter—or even outright scorn!

What few people in the crowd that day realized, however, was that Jesus was deliberately evoking an ancient prophecy from their Hebrew scriptures: "Rejoice greatly, Daughter Zion. . . . See, your king comes to you . . . lowly and riding on a donkey" (Zechariah 9:9). His entry into Jerusalem was evidently, in Jesus' own mind, a moment not for forcing a political agenda but for the fulfillment of prophecy.

Jesus was indeed coming into Jerusalem as its king. Simon Peter had been right to blurt out his suspicion: that Jesus was the "Messiah," the royal anointed King of Israel. Bartimaeus, on the outskirts of Jericho, had been right to keep shouting out that Jesus was the "Son of David" —the long-awaited successor to Jerusalem's first and greatest king. We might well imagine some in the crowd singing, "Hail to you, hail to you, oh David's son! Hail to the Lord's anointed!"

Yet this was a king with a difference. On the one hand, he would turn out to be—at least in the eyes of some, perhaps like Judas Iscariot—so much less than he could have been. This king would not banish the Romans, and the longed-for independent kingdom of Israel would not dawn on the political horizon. Such ardent nationalism would be cruelly disappointed.

On the other hand, he would turn out to be—at least in the eyes of his later apostles, such as Simon Peter or Mary Magdalene—so much more than they had expected, even in their wildest dreams. For this king turned out to be indeed a "returning" king—precisely what the prophet Isaiah had foreseen would be the cause of Jerusalem's greatest joy: "How beautiful on the mountains are the feet of those who bring good news, . . . who say to Zion, 'Your God reigns!' . . . When the Lord returns to Zion, . . . burst into songs of joy together, you ruins of Jerusalem; for the Lord has comforted his people and redeemed Jerusalem" (Isaiah 52:7–9).

In his triumphant entry on Palm Sunday, Jesus was entering Jerusalem, the city of God, as its returning King—indeed, as its Lord and God.

2. JESUS IN BETHANY

There are great views from Bethany of the sun rising over the Dead Sea and the wilderness of Judea. Perched on the slopes of the Mount of Olives, Bethany in Jesus' day was still only a tiny village, the last possible outpost of human habitation before the arid desert soil to the east made vegetation impossible. It was the perfect place to get away from the bustle and stress of the busy city of Jerusalem, located out of sight on the other side of the Mount.

Almost certainly, this is where Jesus and his 12 male disciples slept those first few nights of the week. Each day he would commute into town, teaching in the Temple, but in the evening, he could retreat to this quiet haven. Quite possibly these 13 men were given accommodation in several different homes—after all, they may not all have been able to fit into the home where Lazarus, Martha and Mary lived. Yet on one evening, they evidently took their meal together in the home of a man whom Mark calls "Simon the leper" (quite possibly someone whom Jesus had healed of that dreaded disease).

What happened next took them by surprise: "A woman came with an alabaster jar of very expensive perfume, made of pure nard. She broke the jar and poured the perfume on his head" (Mark 14:3).

In John's Gospel, the woman is explicitly named as Mary, the sister of Lazarus (John 11:2; 12:3). Some have been suspicious why Mark has left her anonymous. This may have been for a very practical reason: To reveal her name would put Mary at risk from reprisals during her lifetime (whereas by the time John's Gospel came to be written, she had since died). And, though the debate continues, this "Mary of Bethany" might also be identified with the "Mary Magdalene" who was first mentioned in Luke 8:2, immediately after the story of a woman shedding her tears and pouring perfume over Jesus' feet.

If this is so, the same woman is now in Bethany performing a similar action—but this time with a deeper purpose. In Galilee her action may have been an impulsive expression of her gratitude to Jesus for rescuing her from her sinful past, an outpouring of her love for having received Jesus' forgiveness (hence Jesus' comment in Luke 7:47, "whoever has been forgiven little loves little").

But now in Bethany, it's something more.

Some wonder if it's just a coincidence that the only other references in the Bible to *nard* or *spikenard* (oil from a plant native to the Himalayas) come in the Old Testament's "love song," the Song of Songs: "While the king was at his table, my perfume spread its fragrance" (1:12; cf. 4:13). Mary's action did not need to be explicitly sexual in order for us to acknowledge it as a powerful expression of love addressed by a woman to a man. This is the nearest, we might say, that Jesus would ever get to experiencing his own wedding and being celebrated, like the kings of old in Psalm 45, as a human bridegroom.

Others rightly wonder if Mary's anointing the head of Jesus was her way of giving Jesus his deserved "coronation" as Israel's true King (after all, the word "Messiah" means the "anointed one"). If so, it was a remarkably brave and potent act—and one that might indeed put Mary in danger from the religious authorities.

Yet Jesus discerned in her symbolic action something even more profound: "She has done a beautiful thing to me; . . . she poured perfume on my body beforehand to prepare for my burial" (Mark 14:6, 8). Jesus was not just Mary's beloved, not just her king—but also the one who would die for her. Her action was not only akin to a royal wedding, but also, simultaneously, to a funeral. It was beautiful but also somewhat bizarre.

Mary, operating from an intuitive understanding that left the male disciples lagging behind, picked up some unspoken signals from Jesus and had now fathomed where he is headed. Behind all the outward, public celebrations, such as his recent triumphant entrance into the city, she detected an inner, private theme of tragedy and looming death. A drama was unfolding for which she had discovered—ahead of all the others—the inner plotline. So she would go through the next few days with this extra, crushing level of insight. And then, when a few days later her intuitions will be vindicated and her worst fears confirmed, she will unsurprisingly wish to be the first to anoint Jesus' body and embalm his precious corpse—for the third and final time.

3. JESUS CLEANSES THE TEMPLE

If Bethany was the place of quiet and private retreat, then the Temple was the place of powerful and public action. This enormous building complex was the very epicenter of Jewish life—its religious heartbeat but, almost inevitably, its political hub as well. The Temple was where Jewish worshippers might come on a daily basis. It was where Jewish pilgrims thronged at each of their four annual festivals. It was also, as we learn from Josephus' writings, where Jewish nationalists gathered throughout the tense decades of Judaism's standoff with Rome. Thus the Temple was a place where riots could develop quickly, causing the Roman soldiers to storm onto the premises from the nearby Antonia fortress in order to quell unrest. This was a place where sparks could fly. Seemingly small actions could have devastating consequences. It would not take much to set the whole thing ablaze.

Located on the site of Solomon's first Temple, which was dedicated around 970 BCE, the whole area had been, for the past 45 years, experiencing a massive renovation program. Around the year 20 BCE, Herod the Great had commissioned a vast expansion of the Temple's platform, requiring enormous stones to be hauled from nearby quarries for the platform's supporting walls. This expansion of the level area on the top meant that there was now around an inner "sanctuary" and a larger outer area known as the "court of the Gentiles"—something which, as a non-Jew, Herod might have hoped to enjoy himself.

But how was this new court of the Gentiles to be used? The high priests had recently allowed a market to develop here. After all, worshippers needed to exchange their ordinary money into the Temple's proprietary currency (the Tyrian shekel) which they could use to pay for sacrificial offerings and to make financial gifts toward the Temple's construction and daily operation. All these transactions had to be conducted somewhere. Why not here?

Jesus disagreed. This is what happened with he returned to the Temple the day after his first arrival:

Jesus entered the temple courts and began driving out those who were buying and selling there. He overturned the tables of the moneychangers and the benches of those selling doves and would not allow anyone to carry merchandise through the temple courts. And as he taught them, he said, "Is it not written: 'My house will be called a house of prayer for all nations'? But you have made it 'a den of robbers'" (Mark 11:15–17).

This famous event, often termed Jesus' "cleansing of the Temple," is widely agreed to be an indisputable event in the ministry of the historical Jesus—even by radical scholars who are otherwise dismissive of the Gospel records. Indeed, many consider it to be the single most important "trigger" precipitating his death. How did he dare?! "By what authority," the religious authorities asked, "are you doing these things? And who gave you authority to do this?" (Mark 11:28). In other words, "Who on earth do you think you are?!"

An understanding had developed, based on the Hebrew scriptures, that there was an intrinsic link between Israel's king and the Temple. Just as David and Solomon had planned and built the Temple, so it would be David's ultimate successor, the Messiah, who would rebuild or restore the Temple. Herod, despite his self-importance and preferred title, the "king of the Jews," had turned out not to have been the long-awaited Messiah.

Almost certainly, Jesus' action was deliberate and intentional, a competing claim to be the authentic Anointed One. Yes, he was concerned about the financial exploitation of the poor. Yes, he was angry that Gentiles were forced to pray amid the noise and evil of a "den of robbers," a phrase drawn from Jeremiah's dire predictions that Solomon's Temple would soon be destroyed. [4]Yet Jesus was also making a point about himself: *He* was the one with the ultimate authority over the Temple. Not coincidentally, he quoted the words of God himself, as conveyed through the prophet Isaiah: "*My* house . . ." Was he implying that this "house," this Temple, really belonged to *him*?

In the opening verses of Mark's Gospel, the Evangelist quotes a prophecy from Malachi to help his readers understand who Jesus was: "I will send my messenger, who will prepare the way for before me" (3:1) the verse begins (Mark sees this as a reference to John the Baptist as the "messenger" who came before Jesus). The prophecy continues: "Then suddenly the Lord who you are seeking will come to his temple." For this Gospel writer, then, there may be layers of meaning beneath Jesus' Temple cleansing—a criticism of commercial wrongdoing, a concern for Gentile access to God, even a warning that the Temple's days are numbered, as in the days of Jeremiah. But for Mark, this layer, too, was not to be missed: Jesus came into the Temple as the "Lord" predicted by Malachi, as its rightful owner. Like a landlord returning to his tenant farm or vineyard, he was looking for faithfulness and fruitfulness—but that was not what he found.

4. JESUS SHARES A MEAL WITH HIS FOLLOWERS

From the dramatic public events in the Temple, we move once more the private and intimate: Jesus having a meal with his disciples, the so-called "Last Supper."

For the many Jewish pilgrims who flocked to Jerusalem, the goal was, if possible, to eat their Passover meal within the walls of the city. Jesus had evidently made some special prior arrangements with the owner of a house who had a guest room that would be large enough for Jesus and the Twelve. This was likely in the southwestern quarter, known as the Upper City, where there were larger houses built for wealthier members of the community. (I have argued elsewhere that the house may have belonged to the father of Mark, the later writer of Mark's Gospel; others that this was one of the places where the female followers of Jesus, such as his mother, had been staying the previous few nights).

But was this really a Passover meal? John's Gospel (13:1) strongly suggests that Jesus' crucifixion took place in the morning *before* the Passover feast began at sunset—that is, during the time when lambs were being slaughtered in the Temple prior to being prepared for the evening meal. And recent examination by astronomers into the lunar calendar in use around the year 30 CE has shown convincingly that John's chronology is likely correct. We conclude that Jesus was celebrating his own distinctive Passover meal a day ahead of schedule. With hindsight, we know why: *24 hours later, he would be dead.*

The disciples probably realized Jesus was planning something irregular, but they were still in for a shock. First, Jesus insisted on washing their feet—something so embarrassing that Peter fiercely objected. And then, midway through the special Passover liturgy (the *Haggadah,* with its recital of the original Passover events in Egypt), Jesus told them the ancient Israelites' "bread of affliction" was now to be understood as his own "body," and that the "cup of redemption" was his own "blood". [5]To good Jews, these suggestions would have been simply horrifying. After all, they never even ate animal meat with the blood still in it; they had been taught that blood represented the "life" that God had given (see Leviticus 17). They certainly were not cannibals eating human flesh! Yet Jesus insisted they all eat and drink—"*all* of you!".[6] Imagine the shock or even disgust on their faces as they passed the plate and then the cup.

From this scene, we conclude that Jesus knew he was about to die; indeed, that he actively intended to bring this fate upon his own head. Moreover, by evoking the Passover story, he was signaling that his imminent death would in due course be understood as a divine act of rescue and deliverance on par with the Exodus. Indeed, it would be an even greater Exodus. In saying those few words— "this is my body . . . this is my blood"—Jesus self-consciously and deliberately placed himself in the age-long sweep of the biblical story and proposed that his death, not the Exodus, was its crowning moment: "Do this in remembrance of *me*!".[7] If one dismisses the claims in the Gospels for this Jesus' eventual resurrection from the dead, one has to conclude that he was a self-deluded fool. And as for his followers, eating the body of their dead hero—they too should be dismissed as sick and benighted. Why celebrate such a macabre meal?

Three days later, when the Gospel of Luke asserts Jesus once again "broke bread" with his disciples on the Emmaus Road,[8] things would begin to make sense. But right now, on this Thursday evening, the disciples must have felt that everything was shrouded in darkness and mystery. Jesus seemed to have a death wish. Why?

For Judas, this was the last straw. If Jesus was not going to be the kind of Messiah Judas wanted him to be—and, worse still, if he was contemplating his own death—then this Jesus should be abandoned to his self-inflicted fate. Thus Judas left the room, heading for the nearby house of Caiaphas, the High Priest.

In due course, the rest of them left too, heading down the steps from the Upper City toward the Siloam Gate. We read that they "sang a hymn"—but one wonders which of them, if any, felt in the mood for singing.

5. JESUS IN GETHSEMANE

Gethsemane in Hebrew means "olive press." This is precisely what one would find at the foot of the Mount of Olives. In Jesus' day it would likely have been a walled-off enclosure in use by local farmers during the day but that at night was suitably guarded. So who let Jesus in?

One possible answer is that a young man called Mark had been told by his father to wait by enclosure's gate and let Jesus enter as soon as he arrived. This makes sense of a puzzling verse about Jesus' arrest found only in Mark's Gospel that refers to a "young man, wearing nothing but a linen garment" (effectively, a nightshirt). When the soldiers tried to seize him, "he fled naked, leaving his garment behind" .[9] Could this be the Gospel's author revealing an embarrassing moment? Effectively, "I was there that night, but I ran away with absolutely nothing on!"

It is likely that Jesus knew he would need privacy, but also that privacy would be hard to find on this night, with thousands of Jewish pilgrims sleeping out all over the Mount of Olives. Hence his probable 'double request' to Mark's father—for use of the upper room for the Passover meal followed by access to his olive-press enclosure.

What time did Jesus reach Gethsemane? He might have needed nearly an hour to get there from the location of Last Supper—walking out through the Siloam Gate and then up the floor of the Kedron Valley. So, we might suggest sometime around 11 o'clock.

And how long was he there? Given that fishermen even today are often able to keep themselves awake all night, it's remarkable that Peter, James and John fell asleep three times. This suggests the arresting party did not arrive until something like 2 o'clock in the morning.

What kept them so long, if Judas went to Caiaphas straightaway? The answer is likely that the High Priest had to make an urgent late-night visit to the Roman governor. The news Judas had brought to him—that Jesus seemed willing to give himself up and would be waiting in a quiet location through the night—had indeed been very welcome. But it left things tight for time. If they went out to arrest Jesus, they had to have confidence he would be dead before sunset the next day, the start of the Passover Festival. If he was not, and they had to keep him in custody for the whole of Passover week, then the people would be in uproar.

The solution was to confirm with Judea's Roman governor, Pontius Pilate, that he would agree to an emergency trial the next morning and then "rubber stamp" the Jewish leader's verdict. Most Passion plays suggest that Caiaphas did indeed make such a visit. In Matthew 27:19 we learn that Pilate's wife, Claudia Procula, had a nightmare about Jesus during the night—quite possibly because her husband told her about Caiaphas' strange request before she went to sleep.

All this political maneuvering went on in the city for two or three hours while Jesus prayed and waited. The fact that he waited so long is yet another sign of his resolute determination to go the way of the cross. If he had chosen, he could easily have walked up the Mount of Olives and, 45 minutes later, settled into bed in Bethany in the home of his friends. How tempting must that have been! But Jesus chose neither to retreat nor to advance, but simply to wait.

"Abba, Father," he prayed, "take this cup from me. Yet not what I will, but what you will".[10]

Here we see Jesus wrestling with God's will, longing with every sinew of his human body for there to be another way. It seems there was none. In speaking about a "cup," picking up the Hebrew prophets' imagery of the "cup of God's wrath" to be drunk by God's enemies,[11] he portended that, during the coming day, he would drink that bitter cup down to its bottommost dregs. No wonder he was in "anguish" and that his "sweat was like drops of blood falling to the ground" (Luke 22:44). Like the olives that earlier in the day had been crushed and pressed nearby—not once but three times—in order to make the finest oil, so Jesus was crushed and pressed in spirit.

At long, long last, Judas and the arresting party arrived; the wait was over. Jesus gave himself up and, after a brief scuffle, nine of the 11 disciples fled up the hill toward Bethany (where they probably stayed for the next 72 hours, fearful to come back into Jerusalem). Only Peter and John followed Jesus, but at a distance. When the main group of disciples looked back, they would have seen a few flaming torches winding toward the Upper City. Their Master was about to be put on trial by the High Priest.

6. JESUS ON TRIAL BEFORE CAIAPHAS

The High Priest's residence was likely one of the largest and most sumptuous houses in the Upper City. Perhaps built on two floors, surrounding a central courtyard, it would have been quite a contrast from the tiny homes Jesus knew so well from Nazareth and around Lake Galilee. Certainly impressive and probably intimidating.

Jesus would have arrived sometime between three and four in the morning. Caiaphas had asked his father-in-law, Annas, to interrogate the prisoner first. Under his questioning Jesus gave little away, suggesting that Annas should interview people who had heard his teaching in public: "I said nothing in secret. . . . Ask those who heard me!" (John 18:20–21).

When Caiaphas and other religious leaders came into the picture, some "witnesses" tried to stick false charges on Jesus—in particular, trying to work out his exact words when he had spoken of destroying the Temple.[12] They recognized that Jesus posed a threat of some kind to the Temple—perhaps setting himself up as an alternative focus of worship for God's people—but they could not get their evidence straight.

At last Caiaphas asked Jesus outright: "Are you the Messiah, the Son of the Blessed One?" Asked a direct question, Jesus answered directly: "I AM! And you will see the Son of Man sitting at the right hand of the Mighty One and coming on the clouds of heaven" (Mark 14:61–62).

Hearing these words, Caiaphas tore his robes. He knew full well the implications of Jesus' words. In the Hebrew scriptures, the "Son of Man" was an exalted figure who the prophet Daniel had envisioned "coming with the clouds of heaven," approaching "the Ancient of Days" and then being ushered into the very presence of God, there to receive "authority and glory" from God, to be "worshipped by people of every language" and to be given a kingdom that would "never be destroyed" (Daniel 7:13–14).

In the ears of Caiaphas, such words were outrageous lunacy and evidence of blasphemy. *Who does Jesus think he is?* Yet they were also exactly the kind of words Caiaphas had likely hoped would come out of Jesus' mouth. Such blatant blasphemy would induce those standing around to agree that Jesus was "worthy of death".[13] According to the Hebrew scriptures, a false prophet leading Israel astray deserved the death penalty. Jesus was clearly just such a false prophet, threatening to corrupt the people of Israel.

Strictly speaking, trials at night-time were illegal under Jewish law. The Gospels clarify that, though Caiaphas' interrogation probably started before dawn, a full and proper meeting of the "whole Sanhedrin" took place "very early in the morning" or "at daybreak" (Mark 15:1; Luke 22:66). Bleary-eyed men would have arrived at the High Priest's house to find the prisoner had already been effectively condemned; but here now, they ratify that judgment with the necessary vote and hurriedly prepare their case for Jesus' next trial—this time before Pilate.

7. JESUS ENCOUNTERS HUMAN EVIL AND FAILURE

For the sake of the timetable, authorities had to keep things moving. Jesus' case was passed from Annas to Caiaphas, from a small group in the High Priest's house to a meeting of the full Sanhedrin, on to Pontius Pilate, to Herod Antipas and then back again to Pilate—all in a matter of four or five hours.

Throughout that awful night, Jesus had no sleep. He was also on the receiving end of verbal mockery and physical abuse. The Gospels tell us an official slapped Jesus in the face for speaking to the High Priest with what he thought to be insolence[14] and that Temple guards blindfolded him and taunted him, saying "Prophesy! Who hit you?!" (Luke 22:64). (It's possible Jesus received the traditional Jewish punishment of 39 lashes, which the apostle Paul would later claim to have received no less than *five* times; see 2 Corinthians 11:24. However, time constraints may have meant Jesus did not receive the full force of religious law in that way. Administration of "justice" may have been left to the Roman authorities.)

Later, Herod's soldiers would ridicule and mock him and Pilate would order him to be flogged, not just *after* his sentencing but even *before*. The Roman soldiers fulfilled this command, adding cruel insult to injury by draping a purple robe on him, crowning him with thorns, and paying mock homage to him as "king of the Jews" .

What was exposed on that day was not the wrongdoing of particular Jewish or Roman guards but the dark material of all our human hearts: our compunction to exploit, abuse and demean those under our power and deny their human dignity—the precise opposite of what Jesus had taught: "Do to others what you would have done to you" (Matthew 7:12).

There were other human weaknesses exposed that night: the failed bravado of Peter and Judas' confused remorse. Entering into their stories, we find that any one of us might have found ourselves in their shoes.

In the story of Judas we see how we too can turn against our friends. We can be so offended when others do not fall in line with our preferred agenda that we sacrifice them on the altar of our plans. We can be tempted by promises of money or favor to abandon our own integrity.

In Peter's story we see how we too can falsely trust our own strength and resolve. We can assume the only way to achieve things in life is to "fight our corner." We can make fine-sounding promises but fail to deliver.

But we can also take encouragement from a key sentence in Luke's account. Just after Peter denied any knowledge of Jesus for the third time, we read: "Just as he was speaking, the rooster crowed. The Lord turned and looked straight at Peter. Then Peter remembered the word the Lord had spoken to him: 'Before the rooster crows today, you will disown me three times.' And he went outside and wept bitterly (Luke 22:60–62).

One can only imagine what Peter felt at that moment, looking into the eyes of Jesus, his friend and Master. His failings were fully exposed —yet from all we know of Jesus, it is not a leap to suggest that Jesus' eyes communicated not dismissive judgment but kindness and understanding. Right then Peter may not have been able to make sense of it. But in the coming weeks, Jesus would give him opportunities to know the risen Lord's continuing love in spite of the disciple's failings.

Encountering Jesus' knowing eyes began a process of forgiveness and healing—something which, if the message of the New Testament is to be believed, can become a reality for everyone. His experience gave Peter confidence some 30 years later—pondering the significance of that night's traumatic events and their implications for all people—to write about Jesus in his role as the good shepherd who brings forgiveness to any wayward sheep snared by evil and failure: "When they hurled their insults at him, he did not retaliate; when he suffered, he made no threats. Instead, he entrusted himself to him who judges justly. 'He himself bore our sins' in his body on the cross; . . .'by his wounds, you have been healed.' For 'you were like sheep going astray,' but now you have returned to the Shepherd and Overseer of your souls" (1 Peter 2:23–25).

8. JESUS ON TRIAL BEFORE PONTIUS PILATE AND HEROD

For some time, it has been thought that Jesus was presented for trial before Pontius Pilate in the Roman army barracks just to the north of the Temple. The Antonia Fortress, named in honor of Mark Anthony, would have housed hundreds of Roman soldiers, deployed to keep an awkward peace in the Temple precincts and elsewhere. It would have been a secure place for Pilate to stay during the few times each year when he needed to visit the turbulent city.

Yet there is another option: the luxurious palace that now-deceased Herod the Great had built some 40 years earlier. This site was equally secure and had the added advantage of a location just inside the city's western wall. With its own private gate, Pilate's entourage could get into Jerusalem without having to risk going through any of its streets.

Modern archaeologists believe they have found evidence for such a gate, which suggests the setting for that Friday morning's trial. The religious leaders, not wanting to defile themselves before the Passover by entering the governor's pagan palace (the *Praetorium*), may have come through that gate to an inner gatehouse courtyard, where they could below the stairs to the palace proper. The platform at the top of the stairs could be identified with the place mentioned in John's Gospel, *Gabbatha*, an Aramaic word for a "stone pavement" (19:13), the location of Pilate's judgment seat. From here Pilate could easily have taken Jesus to a nearby room for private conversation, which he did at least twice (John 18:33–38; 19:8–12).

If this is the right setting, then we can estimate from there the size of the crowd on that Friday morning—for space in such a gatehouse courtyard would have been strictly limited. Even if all 70 members of the Sanhedrin came *en masse*, how many ordinary people would have joined them? Especially so early on this important day of Passover preparation; many men, as leaders of their Jewish households, would have been busy collecting their lambs from the Temple for their evening meal.

Given that the authorities were fearful of the masses, they likely would have wanted as few people as possible to know what they were up to. Perhaps they cajoled a few miscreants to join them, who could be relied on to support their cause, but the total number of people is unlikely to have exceeded 100, and possibly less. This crowd would thus have been a very different group of people from the one that welcomed Jesus a few days earlier. The actions of this tiny group cannot be attributed to an entire people group—despite many horrid anti-Semitic accusations in subsequent centuries.

Whatever the case, Jesus was brought before Pilate perhaps around 7 o'clock in the morning or soon after. Asked by the Roman governor to detail the charges (in Latin, the *accusatio*) the religious leaders answered, "We have found this man subverting our nation"[15]—in other words, he is a false prophet who is leading Israel astray. Yet this religious *accusatio* might not on its own lead to a death sentence, so they continued in a more political direction: "He opposes payment of taxes to Caesar"—readers of the Gospels know this is a lie—"and he claims to be Messiah, a king" (Luke 23:2).

Now *that* should cause Pilate some concern!

Questioning Jesus privately about his supposed "kingdom" (John 18:33–37) Pilate became convinced that Jesus was not the kind of king he or his bosses in Rome needed to trouble themselves about. But then Jesus' accusers mentioned that he had started stirring up trouble first in Galilee, before he had come to Judea. This information offered Pilate the pass-the-buck clause for which he must have been hoping: He promptly sent Jesus off to be tried instead by Herod Antipas, son of Herod the Great, who still ruled over the region of Galilee more than 30 years after his father's death.

Herod may have been staying in the Hasmonean Palace, named after the dynasty that had ruled Judea during a century of Jewish independence (140–37 BCE). The palace was not far—thus, 20 minutes or so later, Jesus stood trial yet again.

This was the Herod Antipas who had ordered John the Baptist's execution and who, when he heard about Jesus' increased popularity in Galilee, began to wonder if John was somehow "back from the dead" (see Matthew 14:2). He had let it be known he wanted to kill Jesus; when Jesus sent his reply, he called Antipas a wily "fox" (see Luke 13:31–32).

Jesus would not get a fair trial here, either. In fact, after plying him with questions, Herod was more interested in getting Jesus to perform a stunt miracle than in getting the truth. When a miracle did not materialize, Antipas instructed his soldiers to ridicule and mock the prisoner. His prime goal was not a quest for truth and justice but rather frivolity and laughter. It was a mockery of a trial in every sense of the word.

Jesus' trials rank among the most disturbing scenes in the Gospels: plot and counter plot, accusations and rejoinders, blame-shifting between Jesus' accusers, shouting and rabble-rousing, political machinations and religious rancor—it all went on around Jesus as he stood there, calm and knowing, in its midst.

At this distance in time, the task of reconstructing a coherent sequence of events is a challenge, because each of the Gospel writers emphasizes different events, encounters and conversations.

- Mark's account is the shortest; indeed, it is so brief (containing just five quick questions from Pilate) that, if it were taken comprehensive, the trial would have lasted less than two minutes!
- Matthew uses Mark's account as a template but then adds

information about Pilate's wife's dream and the governor's handwashing.
- Luke alone mentions Jesus' trial before Herod Antipas and specifies that Pilate declared Jesus' innocence three times.
- John's account is the longest and includes private conversations between Pilate and Jesus, as well as more precise details about times and places—all of which suggest it is eyewitness testimony from Jesus' disciple John (the only male disciple to witness Jesus' trial and execution).

Differences between the Gospel accounts do not require readers to dismiss them, but rather to value multiple perspectives that, taken together, allow us more perspectives to the original event than a single account would give.

9. JESUS IS SENTENCED TO DEATH

The Gospel writers are each convinced that Jesus was innocent of all political charges levied against him. If he was Messiah—a claim they each strongly affirm—he was a quite different Messiah from someone like Barabbas, a political insurrectionist. In fact, a Jewish nationalist agenda was something Jesus had warned people against. Yet here before Pilate, in a deep irony, he would take Barabbas' place and be condemned to die on a cross—the punishment Romans meted out expressly for political rebels. Paradoxically, Jesus would not *speak* in favor of Jewish nationalism but he would end up *dying* for it.

Many of the crisscrossed machinations played out that day relate to confusion about the nature of Jesus' Messiahship. The general

Jewish populace longed for a nationalist Messiah. Caiaphas and his fellow Sadducees on the Sanhedrin, on the other hand, tried to suppress nationalist ardor to curry favor with the Roman authorities (whose presence they still fiercely hated). When Jesus revealed himself to Caiaphas as the exalted "Son of Man"—a mysterious personage presumed to be *greater* than a mere *human* Messiah—this placed the Sanhedrin in an ironic situation, given their opposition to nationalism: This prisoner was *not*, after all, the anti-Rome "political Messiah" they opposed, but he *was* guilty—unless his claims were true (which was, of course absurd!)—of religious blasphemy, which required the death penalty under Jewish law.

Here's the irony: Since 6 CE, the Sanhedrin had lost its right to execute religious criminals. If they wanted him dead, they would have to take Jesus to the Roman authorities—but blasphemy was *not* a crime under Roman law. What *was* criminal according to Rome was the claim to be a political, nationalist Messiah! Thus we understand the Sanhedrin's attempts to hoist on Jesus a charge of anti-Roman activities—even though they knew *Jesus was not a political Messiah.*

Pilate saw through the ploy, surmising that what drove the Sanhedrin's determination was "envy" or "self-interest" (Mark 14:9). Yet the Roman governor still refused to do the right thing: Even though he saw that Jesus was innocent of the charge levied against him, Pilate callously sentenced punishment (Luke 23:16) and ordered him flogged during the trial (John 19:1–3). Pilate was no lover of justice, and he was given to brutal abuse of his power. In fact, in 36 CE his savage butchery in response to a Samaritan revolt would so shock the Roman emperor, Caligula, that Pilate would be deposed from office and ordered back to Rome.

No one in the drama surrounding Jesus emerged with honor or integrity. Everyone was tainted with self-interest and dishonesty. Everyone played games and passed the buck. Jesus was surrounded by human evil in all its forms.

What we see play out in these courtroom scenes is a portrait writ large of our human nature: the worst of us, which often lies buried deep in our hearts, now bursting forth like a volcano, erupting for all to see.

10. JESUS IS CRUCIFIED

Jesus was led from Pilate's *Praetorium* to a place of execution known in Aramaic as *Golgotha,* the "place of the skull" (later translated into Latin as "Calvary"). The precise location of these two sites has been debated through the centuries. If, as argued above, Pilate was staying that weekend in the palace of the former King Herod the Great, and if we accept the traditional site of Golgotha (now marked by the Church of the Holy Sepulchre), then the distance them would have been only a few hundred yards.[16] Jesus would have gone out through what Josephus later called Jerusalem's "Second Wall," using the *Gennath* ("Garden") Gate, and was soon brought to a disused quarry, an area of about 50 yards square.

Many years earlier, stonemasons had left this area to go wild. Bare rocks had gradually been covered by soil, and rough vegetation and wildflowers had grown up, creating a kind of garden in some parts of the quarry. Masons had left a small outcropping of rock, about 15 feet high and 20 feet in diameter, standing in the middle of the quarry—most likely because the limestone was cracked, making it useless as masonry. This small knoll or hillock may have looked like a human skull, giving rise to "Golgotha"; alternately, the name may simply have come about because the quarry was used as a place of execution.

In any event, Golgotha was a convenient place. The Romans liked crucifixions close to main roads so that passersby would get the message: This is what happens to rebels. Mark's Gospel refers to an African man, Simon of Cyrene, forced to carry Jesus' crossbeam (or *patibulum*) simply because he was "passing on his way in from the country" (15:21). Passover visitors and local shoppers going about their business—some carrying water jars fresh from cisterns cut under one side of the quarry—could not have missed the grisly scene. Among the witnesses were Jesus' own friends: the disciple John, Jesus' mother, and a good number of his female followers.

By tradition, Jesus, together with two other criminals, was crucified at the top of a hill. Yet the Gospels never specifically mention a "hill," simply referring to the "place" of Golgotha. So, quite possibly, these crucifixions (which required some space between them) took place on the floor of the quarry—whether near the base of the small hill or even 40 yards away on the other side of the quarry.

"And they crucified him" (Mark 15:24). Mark's account is matter-of-fact: In just 15 verses he covers the *titulus* ("the King of the Jews"), the sneering comments of passersby, the strange darkness at midday, Jesus' quotation from Psalm 22:1 ("My God, why have you forsaken me?") and the Roman centurion's final declaration: "Surely this man was the Son of God!"

Despite what these events must have meant to the first followers of Jesus, Mark's account does not develop the *pathos* of the scene in order to elicit strong emotion; nor does he comment on its ugly brutality. Even the fact that Jesus almost certainly hung on the cross completely naked—shameful in Jewish culture—is only hinted at by Mark's reference to soldiers casting lots for his clothes.

Two other Gospel writers are also quite restrained: Matthew adds a reference to an earthquake at the moment of Jesus' death; Luke portrays a conversation between Jesus and one of the other crucified criminals. John alone is left to add editorial comments and include a little more emotional color—in particular, describing the heartbreaking moment when Jesus says goodbye to his mother, entrusting her to John's care.

Jesus would have hung on the cross for two or three hours, writhing and groaning in agony; throughout that time, Jesus' followers watched him slowly die. Words simply fail to describe the misery of those hours. To watch a friend die in such painful and shameful circumstances would be bad enough; how much worse when that friend had spoken the truth, used his powers to do good and inspired you to pin your own faith and hope on him? Now the embodiment of truth and goodness was being executed; faith and hope were slaughtered before your eyes.

After he breathed his last, Jesus was taken down from the cross and given some preliminary embalming by Nicodemus and Joseph of

Arimathea. They had to act quickly: Sunset, the start of the Passover, was approaching. "At the place where Jesus was crucified there was a garden, and in the garden a new tomb in which no one had ever been laid" (John 19:41)—a tomb cut into the cliff escarpment at the quarry's western edge. They laid him there, knowing—as did the women watching from a distance—that the job was hastily done. They likely laid the corpse on a side slab, a temporary place for preparing a body for its final burial in a shaft grave. That would have to be sufficient for now, but more would need to be done Sunday morning. After rolling a stone across the entrance to prevent disturbance by dogs and vultures, the two men spoke to the women, agreed on a plan of action, and went their separate ways—grieving deeply here at the end of their longest day.

11. JESUS APPEARS TO MARY MAGDALENE

Joseph, Nicodemus, and the women must have left the tomb and returned to their homes in Jerusalem weighed down with grief. In other homes, children were excited as they prepared to celebrate the annual Passover meal and the start of a week's holiday—but Jesus' followers must have found it difficult to join in the festivities. The next 36 hours would be the lowest point in their lives: a Sabbath of enforced rest spent in sorrow and sadness. The women might quietly prepare for the moment early Sunday morning when at last they could return to the tomb; but for now, all they could do was grieve.

What happened next would transform their grief into joy and their abject despondency into shouts of praise. All four Gospels, together with the rest of the New Testament, insist that death was not the end for Jesus. The cruel drama of Friday's crucifixion was followed on Sunday by a dramatic demonstration of divine power. As Luke summarizes the matter in the sequel to his Gospel: "After his suffering, Jesus presented himself to them and gave many convincing proofs that he was alive. He appeared to them over a period of forty days and spoke about the kingdom of God" (Acts 1:3). And Simon Peter, writing toward the end of his life, would start his letter by speaking brazenly about a "living hope" that believers might know—all based on "the resurrection of Jesus Christ from the dead" (1 Peter 1:3).

Countless books have been written and endless debates engaged about whether this, the consistent witness of the New Testament writers, can be taken seriously. Surely it is an absurd claim? Perhaps they were speaking figuratively about Jesus' teaching and influence carrying on after his death—a "resurrection" of a spiritual kind? Aren't these claims for a physical resurrection of Jesus' body a result of their living in a pre-scientific era and thus playing fast and loose with the facts of history?

Many things could be said in response to such understandable questions, but for now we simply clarify but one crucial point: The word for *resurrection*, which the New Testament writers use in their claims for Jesus, is a Greek compound word (*ana-stasis*) that refers in its two constituent parts to a physical "standing-up" (*stasis-ana*). Jesus' body was once horizontal, they claim, but then became vertical. His corpse stood up! Everyone in the ancient world agreed with the obvious truth penned by the great Greek playwright Aeschylus: "After the dust has absorbed a dead man's blood, there is no resurrection [*anastasis*]."[17] Some in the Pharisaic sect of Judaism ventured to believe that at the end of time there might be an *anastasis* for the righteous, but no one expected it to happen in the normal course of history. It had never happened before, and no one was expecting it to happen now.

Yet according to the Gospel writers, it did!

Let's return to the story the Gospels tell about that Sunday morning (as told in Matthew 28, Mark 16, Luke 24 and John 20).

Imagine what you might have seen if you'd been standing on the walls of Jerusalem around 6 o'clock . . .

A few women huddled silently together, making their way out the *Gennath* Gate long before most people were awake. You wonder: *Where are they headed at this early hour? What are they carrying, wrapped up in their cloaks?*

Now that it's the first week of April, the rainy season is past. It's promising to be a bright, warm day with crystal-clear skies. Right now, however, with the sun's rays not yet breaking over the crest of the Mount of Olives, it's still bitterly cold and damp.

The small expedition, trying to go unnoticed, makes its way furtively into an area just outside the walls. It had been a disused quarry, but now you can see some vegetation and spring flowers sprouting up. Soon the women disappear from sight, obscured by a small standing outcrop of rock in the quarry that blocks your view.

Less than a minute later, you see two of them running back toward the city gate. They've dropped whatever it was they'd been carrying and are running as fast as their legs can carry them. Minutes later you see more of the women coming back. These slightly older women are not running but walking, distraught—clasping hold of each other as if any one of them might be about to faint.

Your interest is now fully piqued, and you remain standing on the wall, wondering what you might see next. Within five minutes you see two young men running out from the city toward the quarry. The younger steams ahead of the older, who has a bigger frame and struggles with the pace. Moments later, they too walk back toward the city gate. The younger appears cheerful, gesticulating excitedly, but the older man still looks heavy-hearted and perturbed.

You're about to go down to investigate this strange garden for yourself when you catch sight of one of the younger women—one of the two you'd seen running—now going back out. You decide to follow her, but at a discreet distance. A few moments later, hidden from her view by that outcrop of rock, you peer around the corner to see her pacing around in circles in front of a tomb cut into the quarry wall.

"They have taken away my Lord," she screams, "and I don't know where they have laid him!"

Just then a man comes into view, and she starts to beg him: "Sir if you have taken him away, tell me where you have laid him!" She is agitated and desperate, but when she hears him speak a single word—her own name, "Mary"—she turns and falls to her knees. "Master!" she cries. Her body collapses forward, her hair and hands now covering his feet. She has found the person she was looking for. But unless you're very much mistaken, he does not look dead. On the contrary, he looks very much alive!

12. JESUS APPEARS TO HIS FOLLOWERS

There by the tomb where Jesus of Nazareth had been buried on Friday afternoon, Mary Magdalene meets him once again—now gloriously back from the dead.

So began the most extraordinary day in the history of the world.

It had begun in the cool half-light of dawn with comings and goings in and out of Jerusalem as Mary Magdalene, Joanna, another Mary and others had run to Peter and John with news that the tomb was empty.

Then Mary Magdalene, returning to the tomb, was given a dramatic first encounter with the Risen Jesus.

And the day went on to include other such encounters—with a man called Cleopas and his companion as they walked to a nearby village called Emmaus; with Simon Peter (despite his threefold denial of Jesus three days earlier); and eventually, in the evening, with all the disciples and Jesus' other followers gathered in Jerusalem in a discreet location—almost certainly where they had celebrated Passover.

You can imagine the scene. It's about 8 o'clock in the evening, and perhaps 25 people—men and women, young and old (including Jesus' mother)—have now gathered. This is the wider band of Jesus' followers. They have all just been through the worst week of their lives, but now hope is stirring in their midst. In the past hour, coming in one by one under cover of dark so as not to draw attention, each of the nine disciples who had been hiding in Bethany since Thursday night have come, adding to a sense of reunion and growing excitement. All anyone can talk about is the unbelievable tale Mary Magdalene and Simon Peter are telling: "We have seen our Master! He *is* alive!"

Just then, there's a knock at the door. "Could this be *him*?" They open it carefully, only to see Cleopas and his companion, exhausted and breathless after their eight-mile hike back from Emmaus: "We have seen Jesus!" they gasp. "He broke bread with us this afternoon. We even saw the nail marks in his wrists! It really was him!"

That's the picture to have in your mind when you read what happened next:

While they were still talking about this, Jesus himself stood among them and said to them, "Peace be with you."

They were startled and frightened, thinking they saw a ghost. He said to them, "Why are you troubled, and why do doubts rise in your minds? Look at my hands and my feet. It is I myself! Touch me and see; a ghost does not have flesh and bones, as you see I have."

When he had said this, he showed them his hands and feet. And while they still did not believe it because of joy and amazement, he asked them, "Do you have anything here to eat?" They gave him a piece of broiled fish, and he took it and ate it in their presence (Luke 24:36–43).

Luke is describing an event utterly unique and without precedent: a corpse had stood up! Jesus had been raised from the dead! They were not expecting it, in spite of clear hints Jesus had given; and they even still did not believe their own eyes. These were not gullible people out of touch with reality, but real, ordinary people confronted by a completely *new* reality.

Their lives would never be the same. When they went to bed that night—if any of them were able to get to sleep, that is!—they knew they were the precious few who had been given the secret of the universe and the ultimate meaning of human history:

- There was a living God who was actively involved in the world he created.
- He had vindicated Jesus as the supreme Lord of the world.
- The ultimate enemy—death—had been defeated, giving hope to all who believed in this Jesus.
- and there was the possibility, as Jesus himself had told them just a few hours ago in the 'upper room," that people from all nations throughout the world could receive that most amazing and precious gift of all—the 'forgiveness of their sins."

It was as though a whole new world had been born in the last 24 hours!

As we now, 2000 years later, look back on the events of that first Easter Day, many of us sense within them the best news in the world. It was the dawn of a new age, the launch of a new creation, the central point in human history, the moment when God finally revealed his masterplan for the universe. It was a day that, ever since, has had the power to give birth to joy unspeakable and hope unfathomable. Death is dead and life has won! Evil has been defeated and love has conquered! God in Jesus has entered into the valley of the shadow of darkness, has entered fully into the sufferings of our world, and has emerged victorious, assuring us there will be a "welcome home" at the end of the valley because it is *his* light at the end of the tunnel. As Simon Peter would later write to believers: "Praise be to the God and Father of our Lord Jesus Christ! In his great mercy he has given us new birth into a living hope through the resurrection of Jesus Christ from the dead, and into an inheritance that can never perish, spoil or fade" (1 Peter 1:3–4)

Alleluia! Christ is risen! The Lord is risen, indeed. Alleluia!

4

THE 12 TABLEAUS OF THE PASSION PLAY

One of the most distinctive aspects of the Oberammergau Passion Play is the 12 short *tableau* between each act that show 12 different scenes from the Old Testament. For a couple of minutes, the viewer's gaze is fixed on a small mini-stage bedecked with color that portrays an episode from the Hebrew scriptures (for example, Moses at the burning bush or Daniel in the lions' den). The actors stand motionless, the orchestra plays suitably reflective music, and the viewer's imagination is presented with a scene from 3,000 years ago.

These *tableau vivants* ("living images" in English) offer the audience a welcome pause from the intense drama of the Passion story. Yet they also function as a "pause for thought," designed to give deeper insight into the story of Jesus by drawing comparisons between the events of first-century Jerusalem and select episodes from Old Testament history. Viewers can begin to see, for example, how Jesus is like a latter-day Moses: Just as Moses stood up before a tyrant like

Pharaoh and led his people toward the Promised Land, Jesus stands up to the evil oppression of Pontius Pilate and brings his people into a new era of freedom.

Sometimes the comparison is not immediately obvious: What, for example, is the connection between Jesus and the story of Job being comforted by his friends? The following pages are designed to readers make that connection. Each section offers the biblical passage that inspired that particular *tableau* and then a few suggestions for links between the Old Testament event and the story of Jesus. These are not exhaustive; you may be able to think of other comparisons for yourself.

These tableaus are unspoken commentary on the Passion—yet they are also more. They invite us to see the whole biblical narrative, starting in Genesis, as a coherent plotline along which God has been at work to reveal himself at each stage in the long story of his redemptive purposes. Characters in the Old Testament period, the tableaus suggest, were playing their part in a divine drama far bigger than themselves that pointed forward to the moment when Jesus would come onto the stage and assume the story's central and pivotal role.

The tableaus thus help us understand that what happened to Jesus was not random and arbitrary but rather, as the New Testament writers affirm, was part of God's deliberate plan (see Acts 2:23). As we experience the harrowing events of the crucifixion played out onstage, the tableaus remind us God is still in control and, somehow, he will be able to bring good out of this awful evil.

Undergoing his Passion, Jesus may have taken comfort from these very stories. The set director for the Obergammergau Passion Play, Stefan Hageneier, had this flash of insight while constructing the tableau's balsa-wood models in 2019: "I suddenly realized that these stories from the Hebrew scriptures were well known to Jesus himself. He would have been able to compare what was happening to him with what had happened to Joseph, Moses and Daniel. And from these historical images, he could derive new strength for the challenges ahead. Seen in this way, the tableaus give us a window into the mindset of Jesus, an imaginative *entrée* into his thought-world, and an opportunity to be inspired by what inspired him."

Now there's a thought! These 12 tableaus offer us a window into the mindset of Jesus. Let's allow their brief moment on stage to guide us more deeply into the mind and heart of Jesus.

1. THE LOSS OF PARADISE

The Lord God said, "out his hand and take also from the tree of life and eat and live forever" (Genesis 3:22–24).

These words conclude the Bible's foundational story. Adam and Eve, who in Genesis 2 are portrayed as enjoying life in a beautiful garden created for them by God, now find themselves—having disobeyed God's clear instructions not to eat from the "tree of the knowledge of good and evil"—banished from God's presence. Is there any way back?

This sets up one of the major plotlines of the Bible. Is there a way back to the "tree of life," to the Garden of Eden, to the enjoyment of God's blessing? Now that all our human relationships are marred by tension and prone to breakdown, is there any way that love, trust and peace can be restored between us?

As the Bible's dramatic plot unfolds, there eventually appears on the scene a person who seems to embody God's presence and his love, who restores relationships, and who ends up dying on a wooden cross —described later by his followers as a "tree." Could this be the way back? Is Jesus, through all the ugliness of the Passion that reveals the very worst we human beings can do to each other, actually working with a deeper script—doing something that will overturn the sin of Adam and Eve?

2. MOSES LEADS THE ISRAELITES THROUGH THE RED SEA

As Pharaoh approached, the Israelites looked up, and there were the Egyptians, marching after them. They were terrified and cried out to the Lord. Moses answered the people, "Do not be afraid. Stand firm and you will see the deliverance the Lord will bring you today." Then Moses stretched out his hand over the sea, and all that night the Lord drove the sea back with a strong east wind. . . . The waters were divided, and the Israelites went through the sea on dry ground, with a wall of water on their right and on their left (Exodus 14:10, 13, 21–22).

Once safely on the eastern shore of the Sea of Reeds, Moses and the Israelites looked back and sang together of God's great rescue from the hands of evil ruler of Egypt, the Pharaoh: "I will sing to the Lord, for he is highly exalted. The Lord is my strength and my defense; he has become my salvation" [1]

By the time Jesus comes to Jerusalem, this divine rescue has been remembered in the annual festival of Passover for many centuries. Those in the city that week look on Moses as their great leader and savior, the one through whom God had rescued them from a tyrant and brought them into a safe place where they could worship him freely. How they hope God will do that again!

Jesus' followers would look back at the Passion events and conclude that he was performing a new and deeper "exodus"—forging a narrow escape route through the deep waters of death and out the other side. This Jesus, whose very name means "God saves," had become their salvation.

3. THE TEN COMMANDMENTS AND THE GOLDEN CALF

When the people saw that Moses was so long in coming down from the mountain, they gathered around Aaron and said, "Come, make us gods who will go before us." So all the people took off their earrings and brought them to Aaron. He took what they handed him and made it into an idol cast in the shape of a calf. Then they said, "These are your gods, Israel, who brought you up out of Egypt" (Exodus 32:1, 3–4, 6).

This extraordinary episode comes in the midst of the Exodus story. The God of Israel, who had displayed his love and power by rescuing his people from slavery in Egypt, was now about to reveal his character and truth by giving the Ten Commandments to Moses. Even as this happened, the Israelites turned aside from this God in order to worship a golden calf of their own making. They turned from serving the living and active God to an inanimate and powerless idol. Their inner idolatrous hearts were exposed.

As Jesus enters the Temple, the same issue of idolatry comes to the surface. The Temple was supposed to be appointed by the God of Israel as the "place of his Name," the place where his law, given to Moses at Sinai, reigned. But going back at least to the era of Jeremiah, the Hebrew prophets had recognized it could, paradoxically, become a place of idolatry.

So Jesus issues a challenge, calling people back to the worship of the living God. Yet shockingly, from among the Temple's leading officials and priests, emerge some who have their hearts set on things other than God—on financial extortion, on external religious rituals, on personal or political power. It's a sharp moment of revelation, exposing inner hearts of idolatry.

4. HEBREW SLAVES UNDER EGYPTIAN MASTERS

The Egyptians put slave masters over the Israelites to oppress them with forced labor. . .. They made their lives bitter; in all their harsh labor the Egyptians worked them ruthlessly. . .. The Israelites groaned in their slavery . . . and God heard their groaning (Exodus 1:11–14, 23–24).

Having once been slaves in Egypt was an experience that marked the Jewish mindset for centuries to come. Each year at the Passover meal, they looked back to the time when an Egyptian pharaoh, threatened by a potential enemy in his territory, resolved to force the Israelites into slave labor. Yet miraculously, they ardently believed, their God had stepped in to rescue them—overpowering the oppressor, securing their escape and eventually bringing them to a new home, the Promised Land.

That rescue is what Jesus' disciples would have remembered as they sat down to share the Passover meal. It was an ancient story with a modern echo; history was repeating itself. God's people were once again experiencing political and economic oppression. This time they were not in enslaved in Egypt but were oppressed in their own homeland by a Roman "pharaoh." The Jews in first-century Jerusalem would have echoed the complaint voiced by the Israelites in the days of Nehemiah: "We are slaves today, slaves in the land you gave our ancestors" (9:36). They would have prayed earnestly that their God might once again hear their groaning and step in to rescue them—this time, from the hated Romans!

Looking back in later years on their Last Supper with Jesus, those same disciples would come to see it as the time their prayers were answered—but in a deeper and more mysterious way than they had ever dared to imagine. In Jesus, God had indeed stepped again into their world to rescue them—this time, from evil in all its forms.

5. THE CALLING OF MOSES AT THE BURNING BUSH

The angel of the Lord appeared to Moses in flames of fire from within a bush. ... Moses said, "Here I am." . . . The Lord said, "I have seen the misery of my people... So I have come down to rescue them. . .. So now, go. I am sending you to Pharaoh to bring my people the Israelites out of Egypt. I will be with you...I am who I am... Say to the Israelites, 'I AM has sent me to you'" (Exodus 3:2, 4, 7–8, 10, 12, 14)

Moses' encounter with God in a burning bush was a key episode in the way Hebrews told their story of the Exodus from Egypt. Their leader, despite his fears, received a powerful new revelation from Israel's God: He was to be called by a new name ("I AM") and had called Moses to be the human through whom his rescue operation would be affected. Steeled by this extraordinary vision, Moses went back to face the full wrath of Pharaoh—one man standing alone against a whole system of evil.

In the garden of Gethsemane, we see something similar: one man, alone, encountering God in prayer and steeling himself for a daunting mission against evil. Like Moses, Jesus says effectively, "Here I am; I am willing to go your way." As the writer of Hebrews would later affirm: "During the days of Jesus' life on earth, he offered up prayers with fervent tears to the one who could save him from death, and he was heard because of his reverent submission" (5:7). Given what we see next in the garden—Jesus' steely resolve and determination—we can conclude that he indeed receives strength from the great I AM, some assurance that his God will achieve a victorious rescue—for Jesus himself and for his people.

6. THE PROPHET DANIEL IN THE LION'S DEN

They brought Daniel and threw him into the lions' den... At the first light of dawn, the king hurried to the lions' den. . . . He called to Daniel in an anguished voice, "Daniel, servant of the living God, has your God been able to rescue you from the lions?" Daniel answered, "May the king live forever! My God . . . shut the mouths of the lions. They have not hurt me, because I was found innocent in his sight" (Daniel 6:16, 19–22).

Through the biblical story, there were times when solitary individuals —such as Joseph, Moses, or Jeremiah—stood up for their convictions, ready to face the wrath of those with political power.

In this tableau, we see a man called Daniel, a courtier in the palace of the Persian king, Darius, thrown into a den of lions because he has disobeyed a royal edict to worship the king and no other god. Daniel's enemies found him pursuing his daily routine—praying by his open window three times a day to the God of Israel—and reported him to the king. By nightfall, Daniel was sealed in a pit with several lions, while the king—who personally favored Daniel—spent an anxious night wondering if Daniel's trust in God would vindicate him.

Jesus, standing before Annas and then Caiaphas, is following in Daniel's footsteps: one man, who'd been on his knees worshiping God a few hours earlier, has been denounced by former colleagues and now stands trial. Will his innocence be vindicated? Will his trust in God, and his prayers, be answered? Or, if he is thrown into the ultimate pit of death, will his God somehow rescue him from that dark place?

7. THE MOCKING OF JOB

So these three men stopped answering Job. . . . But Elihu, son of Barakel the Buzite, . . . became very angry with Job. . . . Elihu had waited before speaking because they were older. But when they had nothing more to say, his anger was aroused (Job 32:1–2, 4).

The book of Job is a key part of the Hebrew Bible's "wisdom literature," offering an extended meditation on a key question asked by anyone who hopes to believe in a God of love: *Why, if he exists and has power, do innocent people suffer in his world?* Job is portrayed to readers from the opening verse as genuinely innocent in God's sight—"blameless and upright, fearing God and shunning evil" [2], yet calamity is allowed to befall him—at least in part to see if his trust in God will stand the test.

Three of his friends (Eliphaz, Bildad, and Zophar) come initially to commiserate with him; but in time they each begin to remonstrate him, arguing that he *must* be guilty—otherwise, why would he suffer so much? Thirty chapters later, young Elihu adds his fierce "righteous" anger to their remonstration, rubbing salt in Job's already festering wounds. Effectively, all four put their friend on trial. They mocked his protestations of innocence and threw them back in his face.

Jesus is now going through a trial where his innocence is ridiculed. He experiences physical abuse and verbal mockery from soldiers. And, perhaps even worse, he is betrayed by his friends. Jesus is left utterly alone, bereft of companionship, entrusting himself entirely to God. As his friend Peter would later remember: "When they hurled insults at him, he did not retaliate. Instead, he entrusted himself to him who judges justly" (1 Peter 2:23).

8. THE DESPAIR OF CAIN

While they were in the field, Cain attacked his brother Abel and killed him. . . . The Lord said, "What have you done? Listen! Your brother's blood cries out to me. . . . Now you are under a curse. You will be a restless wanderer on the earth." . . . Cain said, "My punishment is more than I can bear. . . . I will be hidden from your presence . . . and whoever finds me will kill me." But the Lord said to him, "Not so; anyone who kills Cain will suffer vengeance seven times over." Then the Lord put a mark on Cain so that no one who found him would kill him (Genesis 4:8, 10–15).

In the biblical account, Cain's murder of his own brother, Abel, is portrayed as the first outworking of the Fall—a tragic insight into the hatred and evil of the human race, which can culminate even in the murder of one's own family members. It encapsulates the brokenness of the human condition, epitomizing what poet Robert Burns called "man's inhumanity to man."

We see this human brokenness throughout the Passion story: the cowardice of Peter, the treachery of Judas, the envy of the high priests, the political calculations of Pilate. This is how we human beings operate: Each of us is Cain. As we watch the characters caught up in the drama of those Jerusalem events, we cannot judge—in a profound sense, *they are us* and *we are them*.

There is a surprising twist at the end of Cain's story: God places a mark of protection on the murderer, an action that speaks loudly of God's grace and forgiveness toward sinful human beings. And we see that forgiveness demonstrated in Jesus. Denied by Peter, betrayed by Judas, and vilified by various rulers, Jesus absorbs all this "inhumanity to man," taking the full brunt on the chin. He shows us another way to be human: overcoming the force of hatred and evil with the greater power of ever-forgiving love.

9. MOSES EXPELLED BY THE PHARAOH

At midnight, the Lord struck down all the firstborn in Egypt, from the firstborn of Pharaoh to the firstborn of the prisoner. . . . There was loud wailing in Egypt. . . . Pharaoh summoned Moses and Aaron and said: "Up! Leave my people, you and the Israelites! Go!" (Exodus 12:29–31).

Moses stood many times before Pharaoh, the omnipotent potentate who ruled the known world, and demanded the release of the Hebrews. He was one insignificant individual, standing alone against an entire system. What hope was there in such a situation? But then the "passing over" of God's judgment induced Pharaoh, who had prevaricated so many times, to change his mind.

Jesus now stands before Pilate and Herod, those with all the political power in the known world. Once again, it's one solitary man standing against an entire system of worldly power. Once again, it's Passover season and God's people are longing for freedom from the pagan oppressor. Is there any hope?

Pilate prevaricates, trying to work out what to do with Jesus that will serve his selfish purposes, but eventually dismisses Jesus to be crucified. Brute force, oppressive political power, has the last word: Apparently "might is right," and hopes of longed-for freedom are built on sand.

Except there is a twist. Three days later, so the Gospel writers assert, divine power revisits the world, bringing an even deeper rescue. A new Passover, so they claim, has been accomplished, bringing vindication for Jesus and all who long for freedom from the oppressive power of evil. Pilate, like Pharaoh before him, is outmaneuvered by an even greater power, full of goodness and truth.

10. JOSEPH INTERPRETS PHARAOH'S DREAM

God called down famine on the land . . . and sent a man before them—Joseph sold as a slave. They bruised his feet with shackles . . . till what he foretold came to pass. The king sent and released him . . . and made him . . . ruler over all he possessed (Psalm 105:16–21).

The story of Joseph, told as a saga in Genesis 37–50, is vital backstory to the Exodus under Moses. A young teenager, despised by his older brothers as an arrogant "dreamer," was sold by them into slavery and transported off to Egypt, where was soon unjustly thrown into prison. Even in that dark place, he yet established his reputation as one able to accurately interpret dreams. In that capacity, he was eventually brought to the royal palace. Pharaoh had had two similar dreams that

Joseph interpreted as a prophecy of seven years of plentiful harvests followed by seven years of severe famine. Duly honored by Pharaoh, he was charged with the task of managing Egypt's food supply.

After so many years of ignominy, this was the moment of Joseph's vindication. But looking forward, it was also the moment when Joseph was established in a position from which he could later rescue his brothers—preventing them from starving to death from the extreme famine. At the saga's conclusion, we hear Joseph speaking words of forgiveness to his brothers: "You intended to harm me, but God intended it for good—to accomplish what is now being done, the saving of many lives" (Genesis 50:20). Their act of hatred turned out to be the means of their salvation.

Setting this powerful paradigm—of divine providence working through human evil—for the story of Jesus helps us see it with new eyes. Jesus, condemned by Pilate, is rejected by humanity. Could that rejection now place him in the position to act as humanity's rescuer?

11. THE SACRIFICE OF ISAAC ON MOUNT MORIAH

"I swear by myself," declares the Lord, "that because you have not withheld your only son, I will bless you and make your descendants as numerous as the stars. . . . Through your offspring, all nations on earth will be blessed, because you have obeyed me" (Genesis 22:16–18).

This divine promise was given to Abraham after he obeyed God's command to offer his only son, Isaac, as a sacrifice—hearing God's call to stop only once Isaac was bound on the altar. Looking up, Abraham saw nearby a ram, caught by its horns in a thicket; the ram took Isaac's place. And Abraham—no doubt mightily relieved at the last-minute reprieve—named that place "the Lord will provide" (Genesis 22:14).

This episode has long been pondered for deeper significance in both Jewish and Christian traditions. At a superficial level, it is indeed strange: God seems to propose a child sacrifice—something later Hebrew prophets denounced as "detestable" in his sight (see Ezekiel 23:36–37).

Yet the first Christians, reflecting on Jesus' crucifixion, soon began to see in this Old Testament story a powerful picture of the Cross. Abraham did what Jesus had done: pursued a path of determined obedience and trusted in God's ultimate provision. In another way, Abraham enacted the role of God, ready to offer as a sacrifice the most precious thing in his sight: his only son. Hence Paul's words describing God's grace: "He did not spare his own Son but gave him up for us all" (Romans 8:32). Seen in this light, Jesus' crucifixion, despite its horror, can be seen as an act of deep love: God graciously provides the sacrifice, his most precious gift: his only Son.

12. SALVATION BY LOOKING UP AT THE BRONZE SERPENT

"Just as Moses lifted up the snake in the wilderness, so the Son of Man must be lifted up, that everyone who believes may have eternal life in him. For God so loved the world that he gave his one and only Son, that whoever believes in him shall not perish but have eternal life" (John 3:14–16).

In conversation with Nicodemus, Jesus gently chides this "teacher of Israel" for not understanding the "heavenly things" he, Jesus, is trying to teach him. One such thing is a strange future event when Jesus would in some way be "lifted up." What could he mean?

Later in John's Gospel, Jesus uses this phrase again: "When I am lifted up from the earth, I will draw all people to myself" (John 12:32). John adds, to make sure no one misses the point: "He said this to show the kind of death he was going to die" (v. 33).

"Lifted up" makes two very different appearances in the Hebrew scriptures. The first, as Jesus told Nicodemus, is Moses' lifting up a bronze snake in the desert. The Israelites, experiencing judgment because of their disobedience, were urged to look up from their suffering to what God was "lifting up" as a means of rescue. "Look at my crucifixion," Jesus was saying, "and you will find it a place of healing and rescue."

The second appearance of "lifted up" can be found in the prophecies of Isaiah: In an opening vision the prophet sees the Lord "high and exalted" (6:1) and then later sees God's servant being "lifted up and highly exalted" (52:13). Based on this second reference to the Hebrew scriptures, John understands Jesus' being "lifted up," in spite of its shame and indignity, as a place of God's exalted glory. On the day of the crucifixion, John may have seen only tragedy and disgrace—but in hindsight and guided by these biblical insights, he came to see it as the revelation of God's loving rescue and dazzling glory.

ABOUT THE AUTHOR

Dr. Peter Walker studied Classics and Early Church History at Cambridge University and has done extensive research at post-doctoral level on attitudes toward Jerusalem in the time of both the Bible and the Early Church. For many years, he taught New Testament Studies at Wycliffe Hall at the University of Oxford and was for five years Professor of Biblical Studies at Trinity School for Ministry near Pittsburgh, Pennsylvania.

Dr. Walker has led guided tours to the lands of the Bible for more than 30 years. He has written a dozen books and numerous articles on Jesus, the New Testament, and the Holy Land today. Peter is an ordained clergyman in the Church of England. He and his wife, Georgie, live in the United Kingdom and have two married children.

FURTHER READING

If you have enjoyed the Passion Play and would like to look more closely at the story of Jesus as described in the Bible, Dr Peter Walker has written some other books which you might find helpful:

Jesus and His World

(Lion Hudson, Oxford 2003)

Your introduction to the historical Jesus, viewing his life and ministry against the background of his first-century Jewish world.

In the Steps of Jesus: An Illustrated Guide to the Places of the Gospels

(Lion Hudson, Oxford 2003; revised color second edition, 2021)

An overview of Jesus' life, taking you through each of the places he visited and giving you all the archaeological and historical information you need about those places before and since.

In the Steps of Paul: An Illustrated Guide to the Apostle's Life and Journeys

(Zondervan, 2008)

A similar overview of Paul's life, taking you through each of the places he visited—from Damascus to Rome.

The Lion Guide to the Bible

(Lion Hudson, Oxford 2010)

A friendly "companion" to guide you through the whole Bible, giving you a brief summary of each of its 66 books, with helpful maps and diagrams of biblical history and geography.

The Story of the Holy Land: A Visual History

(Lion Books, Oxford 2018)

An overview of the history of the Holy Land, taking you on a journey from the days of Abraham to the present day, complemented by lavish photographs.

The Jesus Way: Learning to Live the Christian Life

(Monarch, Oxford 2020)

Based on two Bible stories (in Luke 24 and Acts 2), an introduction to Christian discipleship, giving 12 key steps for those wanting to be Jesus' followers today.

REFERENCES

A NOTE FROM THE PUBLISHER

1. *In the Steps of Jesus: Gospels* (full color edition: Oxford: Lion Hudson, 2021).

3. THE FIRST PASSION STORY

1. Mark 11:11
2. Luke 19:11
3. Luke 20:9-19
4. Jeremiah 17:11
5. Matthew 26:26
6. Matthew 26:27
7. Luke 22:19
8. Luke 24:13-35
9. Mark 14:51
10. Mark 14:36
11. Isaiah 51:22
12. Mark 14:57-58
13. Mark 14:64
14. John 18:22
15. Luke 23:2
16. For fuller arguments, see my books *The Weekend that Changed the World* and *In the Steps of Jesus.*
17. Aeschylus, *Eumenides*, trans. by Herbert Weir Smyth, rev. by Cynthia Bannon and Gregory Nagy, Harvard University Center for Hellenic Studies, Aug. 11, 2019. https://chs.harvard.edu/CHS/article/display/5298 (accessed December 2020).

4. THE 12 TABLEAUS OF THE PASSION PLAY

1. Exodus 15
2. Job 1:1

Made in the USA
Las Vegas, NV
19 February 2022

44244602R00059